Masterpieces: Artists and Their Works

Van Gogh

by Shelley Swanson Sateren

Consultant:
Joan Lingen, Ph.D.
Professor of Art History
Clarke College
Dubuque, Iowa

Bridgestone Books
an imprint of Capstone Press
Mankato, Minnesota

Bridgestone Books are published by Capstone Press
151 Good Counsel Drive, P.O. Box 669, Mankato, Minnesota 56002
http://www.capstone-press.com

Library of Congress Cataloging-in-Publication Data
Sateren, Shelley Swanson.
    Van Gogh/by Shelley Swanson Sateren.
    p. cm.—(Masterpieces: artists and their works)
    Includes bibliographical references and index.
    Summary: Discusses the life, works, and lasting influence of Vincent van Gogh.
    ISBN 0-7368-1124-9
    1. Gogh, Vincent van, 1853–1890—Juvenile literature. 2. Painters—France—
Biography—Juvenile literature. [1. Gogh, Vincent van, 1853–1890. 2. Artists. 3. Painting,
Dutch. 4. Art appreciation.] I. Title. II. Series.
ND653.G7 S33 2002
759.9492—dc21   2001003745

Editorial Credits

Blake Hoena, editor; Karen Risch, product planning editor; Heather Kindseth, cover and
    interior layout designer; Katy Kudela, photo researcher

Photo Credits

Art Resource/Musee d'Orsay, Paris, France, cover (right); Van Gogh Museum, Amsterdam,
    The Netherlands, 4, 12; Erich Lessing/Musee d'Orsay, Paris, France, 8 (top)
Don Eastman, cover (left)
Roget Viollet/Getty Images, 10 (bottom)
Kunsthaus, Zurich, Switzerland/Bridgeman Art Library, 10 (top)
Musee d'Orsay, Paris, France/Giraudon-Bridgeman Art Library, 20
National Gallery, London, UK/Bridgeman Art Library, 14
Philadelphia Museum of Art/CORBIS, 8 (bottom)
Private Collection/Bridgeman Art Library, 6
Rijksmuseum Vincent Van Gogh, Amsterdam, The Netherlands/Bridgeman Art Library, 18
The Barnes Foundation, Merion, Pennsylvania, USA/Bridgeman Art Library, 16

1 2 3 4 5 6 07 06 05 04 03 02

Table of Contents

Vincent painted *Self Portrait with Straw Hat* in 1887. His art style influenced Expressionism.

Vincent Van Gogh

Vincent Van Gogh (1853–1890) sold only one painting during his lifetime. Like many artists, he did not become famous until after his death.

Vincent became an artist when he was 27 years old. He died 10 years later. In that time, he created more than 1,000 paintings and drawings. He sometimes completed a painting in one day.

Vincent tried to show emotions through his art. He often painted farmers and miners. He wanted to show the struggles of these working people. Vincent also had a unique painting style. His thick, curved brush strokes showed movement and excitement. This style of painting influenced Expressionism. During this art movement, people tried to show feelings in the art they created.

After his death, artists and art critics began to praise Vincent's work. People began to buy his paintings. Today, Vincent is one of the world's most famous painters. His paintings sell for millions of dollars.

Vincent made this charcoal drawing, *Portrait of Theodore Van Gogh*, of his father in 1881. It shows his father's seriousness.

Young Vincent

Vincent Willem Van Gogh was born in Groot Zundert, Holland, on March 30, 1853. His parents were Theodore and Anna Cornelia Van Gogh. His father served as the minister for the small farming village where they lived.

Vincent was the oldest child in his family. He had three sisters and one brother, Theo. Theo was Vincent's closest friend. Vincent sometimes drew sketches of animals and plants that they saw while playing outside.

Vincent was a stubborn child. His moods often changed. Vincent's parents thought he was a difficult child. They believed he had rude manners. Vincent's behavior created problems for him throughout his life.

Vincent's parents sent him to a boarding school when he was 12 years old. They wanted Vincent to learn how to act and dress like a gentleman. But he did not keep himself or his clothes tidy at school. He also argued with other students. At age 15, Vincent left school to find a job.

Vincent learned how to paint by copying Millet's works in his own style. *La Siete, d'apres Millet,* or *The Meridian* (top) is Vincent's painting. Millet painted *Meridian* (bottom).

Early Influences

In 1869, Vincent began to work as an assistant for an art gallery. He took a job with his uncle's company, Goupil & Cie. His uncle was an art dealer.

At first, Vincent was successful at his job. He enjoyed seeing art and discussing it with other people. In 1873, he moved to London, England, to work for the company's art gallery there.

Vincent eventually became unhappy with his job. He did not get along with other workers. He sometimes argued with customers about the paintings they wanted to buy. In 1876, Vincent decided to leave the company.

While in England, Vincent studied art and books. He admired English writers such as Charles Dickens. Dickens wrote about working-class people.

The French painter Jean-Francois Millet also influenced Vincent. Vincent studied Millet's paintings of peasants working in fields. Soon, Vincent began to draw and paint people at work.

Vincent's letters to Theo included sketches of people he saw. He liked to draw and paint working people such as in *Two Peasants Planting Potatoes* (top).

Borinage

In 1876, Vincent entered school to become a minister like his father. But he had trouble with his studies and failed his exams.

Vincent did not let this failure stop him. In 1879, he convinced church officials to allow him to be a minister in Borinage. This coal-mining region is in southern Belgium.

The coal miners there were very poor. They had little food and lived in wooden shacks. Vincent felt sorry for them. He often gave them his extra clothing and food. But church officials at the time did not approve of these actions. They told Vincent he had to leave his job.

During his time in Borinage, Vincent often wrote to Theo. In his letters, he included sketches showing the miners' struggles.

Vincent began to draw more after he left his job as a minister. He wrote to Theo saying that creating art made him feel less sad and lonely. At age 27, Vincent decided that he wanted to be an artist.

In 1885, Vincent painted *Potato Eaters*. This painting is considered to be his first masterpiece. Vincent used dark colors such as browns and grays in many of his early paintings.

Beginnings as an Artist

In 1880, Vincent moved to Brussels, Belgium, to study art. There, he created many pencil and charcoal drawings of nature scenes and peasants working.

In 1882, Vincent began to experiment with oil paints. He sometimes squeezed paint out of the tube right onto the painting. Vincent was excited about his art. On many days, he painted all day and into the night.

Theo helped Vincent become an artist. Theo sent Vincent money for art supplies. He also sent Vincent art books to study. The money Theo gave him was the only money Vincent had. It was not always enough to buy both art supplies and food. Vincent often went hungry. To him, art supplies were more important than food.

Vincent also was unable to earn money selling his paintings. People did not want to buy paintings of people at work. They wanted to see more pleasant scenes. But Vincent hoped to show people the struggles of the poor.

Sunflowers were Vincent's favorite flowers. He painted seven different versions of *Sunflowers*.

Paris

In 1886, Vincent moved to Paris to live with Theo. In Paris, many artists were experimenting with new styles of art. Vincent wanted to meet these painters and discuss art with them.

At the time, Impressionism was a popular art movement. Impressionists tried to paint scenes as they appeared at a quick glance. These artists used broken brush strokes to do this.

Vincent also became interested in Japanese art while in Paris. Japanese artists used bright colors.

Vincent was greatly influenced by Impressionism and Japanese art. He began to use short, curved brush strokes. He also stopped painting with dark colors and began to use brighter colors. Yellow became one of his favorite colors.

Vincent still could not sell his paintings. He often did not have enough money to hire models whom he could paint. He painted more than 20 portraits of himself.

Joseph-Etienne Roulin was a postman in the town of Arles.
He was one of Vincent's only friends there.

Arles

Living with Vincent was hard for Theo. Vincent made huge messes and often argued. In February 1888, Vincent moved to a small village in southern France called Arles. He wanted to stop fighting with Theo. Vincent also wanted to paint the scenery there.

Vincent continued to paint in bright colors and curl his brush strokes. Their curved shapes added motion and excitement to his paintings. Later, Vincent's style of painting would help influence Expressionism.

Vincent wanted to start an artists' community in Arles. He invited other artists to join him. Only Paul Gauguin visited. Vincent and Gauguin discussed art and painted together. But they often disagreed and argued about art.

After one argument, Gauguin was very mad at Vincent. Gauguin decided to leave Arles. Vincent was so upset that he cut off a piece of his own left ear.

Wheatfield with Crows was one of Vincent's last paintings. Some people believe that the dark sky shows how angry and upset Vincent was at the time.

Illness

Vincent struggled throughout his life. He often did not have money for food. Many experts believe that Vincent suffered from a mental illness. Others believe he may have had epilepsy. He often had attacks during which he did not know what he was doing. Vincent also may have suffered from lead poisoning. At the time, lead was used in paints.

In 1889, Vincent entered a mental hospital to rest. He continued to paint there. But he still had attacks. He also struggled with feelings of sadness and loneliness. Even painting no longer made him feel happy.

In 1890, Vincent decided to move to the village of Auvers near Paris. He wanted to be closer to Theo. In Auvers, Vincent was under the care of Doctor Paul Gachet.

Soon after Vincent moved, he learned that Theo might lose his job as an art dealer. Theo had always given Vincent money. Vincent felt guilty. He felt as if he was a burden to his brother.

Vincent painted this portrait, *Dr. Paul Gachet*, in 1890.
It is one of his most famous paintings.

Vincent Van Gogh's Art

The news that Theo might lose his job upset Vincent. On July 27, 1890, Vincent shot himself. He died two days later. Vincent was 37 years old. Theo was saddened by his brother's death. He died six months later.

Theo's wife, Johanna, took care of Vincent's art and the letters he wrote to Theo. Stacks of Vincent's paintings filled Johanna's apartment. She shared them with museums. She also had Vincent's letters published in books.

About 25 years after Vincent's death, people began to admire his art. Today, he is considered one of the most famous painters of all time. Many museums around the world show his art.

In 1987, Vincent's painting *Irises* sold for $54 million. In 1990, his painting *Dr. Paul Gachet* sold for $82.5 million. These paintings are some of the most expensive ever sold.

Important Dates

1853—Vincent is born in Groot Zundert on March 30.

1857—Vincent's brother, Theo, is born.

1869—Vincent begins to work for Goupil & Cie.

1873—Vincent moves to London.

1879—Vincent becomes a minister in Borinage.

1880—Vincent decides to become an artist; he moves to Brussels to study art.

1886—Vincent moves to Paris to live with Theo.

1888—Vincent moves to Arles; Paul Gauguin visits Vincent; the two artists discuss art and paint together.

1889—Vincent enters a mental hospital in St. Remy, France.

1890—Vincent moves to Auvers.

1890—Vincent dies on July 27.

1891—Theo dies on January 25.

Words to Know

boarding school (BORD-ing SKOOL)—a school where students live during the school year
epilepsy (EP-uh-lep-see)—a mental illness that causes people to have blackouts or convulsions
exhibit (eg-ZIB-it)—a public display of artwork
Expressionism (ek-SPRESH-uh-ni-zuhm)—an art movement in which artists tried to show emotions in their work
Impressionism (im-PRESH-uh-ni-zuhm)—an art movement in which artists painted in broken brush strokes to show a scene the way it looked at a quick glance
peasant (PEZ-uhnt)—a person in Europe who worked on a farm or owned a small farm
sketch (SKECH)—a rough drawing of something

Read More

Connolly, Sean. *Vincent Van Gogh*. The Life and Work of. Des Plaines, Ill.: Heinemann Library, 2000.
Greenberg, Jan, and Sandra Jordan. *Vincent Van Gogh: Portrait of an Artist.* New York: Delacorte Press, 2001.
Holub, Joan. *Vincent van Gogh: Sunflowers and Swirly Stars.* Smart about Art. New York: Grosset & Dunlap, 2001.

Useful Addresses

Montreal Museum of Fine Arts
P.O. Box 3000, Station H
Montreal, QC H3G 2T9
Canada

Museum of Modern Art
11 West 53rd Street
New York, NY 10019

Internet Sites

Van Gogh Museum
http://www.vangoghmuseum.nl
The Vincent van Gogh Gallery
http://www.vangoghgallery.com
Web Museum, Paris—Gogh, Vincent van
http://www.ibiblio.org/wm/paint/auth/gogh

Index